# She Is...

# Devotional Guide

ISBN: 9798744874490

Requests for information should be addressed to:
　The Connection Church
　PO Box 2225
　Kyle, TX 78640

# She Is...

Day 1: *Loved* - 6

Day 2: *Courageous* - 12

Day 3: *Enough* - 17

Day 4: *Influential* - 22

Day 5: *Prayerful* - 28

Day 6: *Equipped* - 34

Day 7: *Fearless* - 39

*Hello Gorgeous,*

I want to take a moment to celebrate you! You are doing it! Being a woman is a divine privilege from God. From the very beginning, in Genesis, God says,

*So God created man in his own image, in the image of God he created him; male and female he created them.*

Genesis 1:27

You were created in the very image of God. That means that you are unique and valuable to the purposes and plans of God.

Did you know that, throughout the bible, kingdom plans were dependent on women? Women like Deborah and Esther were put in places of influence so that God's plans and purposes would move forward. Throughout history, the strength, tenacity, loyalty, and gentleness of women have been significant.

God continues to elevate the abilities and presence of women today.

As mothers and leaders, caregivers and world changers, we have been uniquely and divinely positioned for such a time as this (Esther 4:14). God has given each of us a job, position, resources, education, and more. God has opened opportunities to optimize His kingdom purposes. To miss a kingdom assignment because we've become too caught up in our personal kingdom is one of the greatest tragedies we could ever face.

Here's the best news: You are never alone. As a community of women, we make it a practice to cheer one another on, to be available, and to walk with each other through life's moments.

I'm excited for you as you walk in the roles that God himself has ordained for you as Mothers, Leaders, Caregivers and Friends.

The following pages are full of godly wisdom and encouragement from the Bible to help you discover more about who God has created you to be. May you be filled with His peace and purposes as you spend time with your Creator!

Love You Big,

*Pam Phillips*

# Day 1: Loved

## Today's Verse

*And I pray that you, being rooted and established in love, may have power, together with all the saints, to grasp how wide and long and high and deep is the love of Christ, and to know this love that surpasses knowledge – that you may be filled to the measure of all the fullness of God.* Ephesians 3:17-18

## INSPIRATION

There's no way for us to completely fathom the love that God has for us. That's why we must accept this type of love in faith. God's love for us is beyond our knowledge – we cannot fully understand it! But we don't have to understand it to accept it. There is beauty in the thought that we are deeply loved by our Heavenly Father with a kind of love that goes beyond our knowledge and understanding.

How perfectly wonderful is that?

As a mom, ask God daily for the understanding of His love for you. As moms, we need to realize the depths of God's love more than anyone because we are in the position to teach God's love to the next generation. Think about it: if the next generation was told every single day about the depth of love that God has for them, how would that change our entire culture? It would be a revolution!

You, as the mom in your house, doing the mundane everyday tasks of motherhood, YOU could start a revolution! This revolution would set your child on a course that would change their identity forever. Your child will be so rooted in God's love that even when they fail, they will know they are still loved. When your child doesn't get that promotion at work, he will still know he is loved. The ramifications are endless.

Moms, *"I pray that you, being rooted and established in love, may have power, together with all the saints, to GRASP how wide and long and high and deep is the love of Christ."* Amen!

**Pray this today:**

Oh, how I want to believe this deep, everlasting love that You have for me! God, open my eyes. Help me push against my critical nature and accept Your love for me. God, I want to embrace Your love, so that I may in turn teach my children. I cannot teach what I do not know. I'm asking You today, to give me faith like none other, so I will accept Your deep love for me. In Jesus' name, Amen.

## Beauty Tip

Instead of hopping in the shower to shave your legs, use baby oil.

If you see a patch of hair you missed or need clean shaven legs stat, use baby oil instead of jumping in the shower — or, worse — dry-shaving.

**Did You Know?** You can use coconut oil to remove makeup!

*Easy Meals for Busy Moms*

## Garlic Parmesan Pasta

This One Pan Garlic Parmesan Pasta is a delicious dinner and it's an easy recipe. I love that you place all the ingredients into a pot after you sauté the garlic, and then you let it simmer for 20 minutes until done. Serve it with some bread and a side of vegetables and dinner is on the table. To change up the recipe, you could also add cooked chicken to the top to make it a garlic parmesan chicken pasta dish. Here is how to make the recipe:

### Ingredients

1 tablespoon olive oil

2 tablespoons garlic, minced

2 cups chicken broth

½ cup milk

½ cup heavy cream

2 tablespoons butter

8 oz linguine pasta

½ teaspoon salt

¼ teaspoon pepper

½ cup shredded Parmesan cheese

1 tablespoon parsley, chopped

## Directions:

In a large pot, heat olive oil and add garlic. Cook garlic for 1-2 minutes.

Add in chicken broth, milk, heavy cream, butter, pasta and salt and pepper. Stir and bring to a boil.

Reduce heat to low, cover pot, and simmer for about 20 minutes until pasta is tender. Stir the pasta once or twice during this time.

Remove from heat, add shredded Parmesan cheese and stir to combine. Sprinkle parsley on top. Serve warm.

_____

_____

_____

_____

_____

_____

_____

_____

_____

_____

_____

_____

_____

_____

_____

_____

_____

_____

_____

_____

_____

# *Day 2: Courageous*

## Today's Verse

*For if you remain silent at this time, relief and deliverance for the Jews will arise from another place, but you and your father's family will perish. And who knows but that you have come to your royal position for such a time as this?* Esther 4:14 (NIV)

## Inspiration

How do you define courage? When I think of a woman of courage, I think of Esther from the Bible. If you're not familiar with Esther, I encourage you to do yourself a favor and read the book of Esther.

Here is my version of her story. She is left an orphan, raised by an uncle. She is beautiful, both inside and out. The king chooses her as queen through a grueling selection process. Her uncle is in danger. She is called to rise-up with all the odds against her. What will she do?

In Esther's story, her uncle is an important figure. He's not easy on her. Her doesn't always totally side with her. He asks hard questions. Questions that ultimately lead Esther to take courage and do the right thing, even when she knows all the odds are against her.

We all need a person like that, right? You need that person who has your best interest in mind. You need the one who asks the hard questions. The one who probably gets on your nerves because you don't want to hear it. The person who inspires you to "take courage" and do the hard thing.

Taking a step that requires courage is more likely if we surround ourselves with the right people. Look around. Do you have these kinds of people? If you do, thank God for them. If you don't, I encourage to pray for these kinds of people in your life.

**Pray this today**

Lord, you gave Esther her uncle and you gave her the courage to make hard decisions. I ask for these kinds of women in my life. Women who have my best interest and are willing to say hard things in love. And women who will walk with me through difficult decisions. Also, help me as I take steps that require courage, having faith that you have equipped me with all that I need. I want to be a woman of courage. In Jesus' name, Amen.

## *Beauty Tip*

Dry nail polish quickly by dunking nails in ice water.

Let them air dry for a couple minutes then dunk away.

NOTE: Although ice water helps the surface dry quickly, your polish can still get messed up if you're not careful. We recommend you only dip, not swirl.

## *Easy Meals for Busy Moms*

## Pastor Pam's Roast, Potatoes & Carrots

If you're looking for a hearty meal that can turn into tomorrow's lunch, this is it!

**Ingredients:**

Chuck Roast (the size appropriate to feed your family)

10-12 medium Russet Potatoes (peeled and chunked)

1 small bag of baby carrots

½ yellow onion

1 package of brown gravy mix (I use the H-E-B brand)

Garlic salt

Salt & Pepper

**Directions:**

Remove your Roast from the packaging and place it in your crockpot. Liberally season both sides with garlic salt.

Mix your brown gravy pkg. with 1 cup of water and pour over roast.

Place cut up onion slices on top of the roast.

Put potato chunks and carrots on top.

Salt & pepper the veggies

Put the lid on and cook on low for 6-8 hours until roast is tender and falling apart!

If you have leftovers, eat it the next day on bread. It makes a great Roast Beef Sandwich!

_____

_____

_____

_____

_____

_____

_____

_____

_____

_____

_____

_____

_____

_____

_____

_____

_____

_____

_____

# Day 3: Enough

## Today's Verse

*His divine power has given us everything we need for life and godliness through our knowledge of him who called us by his own glory and goodness. 2 Peter 1:3*

## Inspiration

Many times, as moms we feel inadequate. We feel that we don't have enough patience, unconditional love, endurance, strength, or courage to discipline in love. How refreshing to know that through Jesus, God has given us everything we need to walk this journey!

Whether you're home all day with small children, or juggling a full-time career with teenagers, we all need endurance for the challenges of parenting.

Ask Jesus to give you strength as you battle your strong-willed child or your child that is painfully shy and awkward around others. Ask God to teach you how to meet your child where he/she is and to lovingly teach them how to socialize. Ask Jesus to give you the courage to discipline your children, and even though it is hard and painful, that you would discipline them in love to set them up for success in their future.

You don't have to "try" to be a better mom. You already have everything you need. Just go to the source... Jesus.

**Pray this today:**

Thank you, Lord, for giving me everything that I need to walk this road of motherhood. God, I feel inadequate almost every day as a mom. But I know that through you, I am not inadequate; I have everything I need. Thank you for that. Remind me throughout my day to lean on you. In Jesus' name, Amen.

*Beauty Tip*

Deep condition your hair before you exercise.

Before you go to the gym, apply a deep conditioner to your hair and then put it up into a bun. The time, and the heat from your body, will help the conditioner set in.

**NOTE:** Limit your workout to less than an hour. Leaving moisturizer in for longer could lead to over-conditioned hair, eventually making it more prone to breakage.

## *Easy Meals for Busy Moms* French Bread Pizza

### Ingredients

1 loaf French Bread

½-3/4 cup Tomato Sauce

2-3 cups Mozzarella cheese, shredded

Basil

Garlic Salt

Any toppings you like on your pizza such as pepperoni, olives, tomatoes, bell peppers, onions and pineapple

## Directions

Preheat oven to 400 degrees.

Slice French bread loaf in half lengthwise.

Spread tomato sauce on each half of the bread then sprinkle basil and garlic salt on top of the sauce.

Sprinkle cheese on the bread and cover with your favorite toppings.

Bake for 10-15 minutes until cheese is melted.

_____

_____

_____

_____

_____

_____

_____

_____

_____

_____

_____

_____

_____

_____

_____

_____

_____

_____

_____

_____

_____

# Day 4: Influential

## Today's Verse

*I have been reminded of your sincere faith which first lived in your grandmother Lois and in your mother Eunice and, I am persuaded, now lives in you also.*

2 Timothy 1:5

## Inspiration

The influence of a mom is like no other. Our influence impacts generations to come. The legacy a mom leaves behind doesn't only affect her child, but many future generations. Therefore, as a mom, take notice of how you are influencing. Are you passing along bad habits, a quick temper, and a sense of entitlement? Or are you passing along love and grace-reflecting Christ in your daily walk, showing your children how different your life is because of Christ?

In this verse, Lois and Eunice had lives which exhibited God's love and faith. The way they loved their families was so noticeable to the outside world that New

Testament author Timothy wrote about them. You could have this kind of effect on your family.

Keep in mind the kind of love and faith exhibited by Lois and Eunice only comes from God. Don't try to do it in your own strength. If you do, you will be frustrated and left feeling like you cannot do it. Lean in on God; ask Him to give you what you need to love your child. Read God's word on a daily basis and walk with Him. The first step, however, is to start noticing what type of legacy you are leaving behind.

**Pray this today:**

I want to leave a legacy of sincere faith and love. God, I would love for my great-grandchildren to know me for my strong faith in You and to know that I loved people because You loved me. God, teach me. I know I am weak in this area-I lose my temper, I am impatient with my children, I get frustrated and aggravated quickly. Fill me up with Your love, Your grace, Your faith-to the point where it overflows from me onto those that I love. In Jesus' name, Amen.

*Beauty Tip*

HAIR: Use dry shampoo after washing your hair to boost volume.

Instead of digging through your stash of hair products or teasing hair, just apply dry shampoo after you've just washed and dried your locks. It will help remove any leftover oils that cause excess weight.

If your hair is staticky, instead of loading it up with products, grab a dryer sheet and run it through your hair wherever there is static. Bonus: Your hair will smell amazing

*Easy Meals for Busy Moms*

## One Skillet Mexican Rice Casserole

**INGREDIENTS:**

1 small red onion, diced

1 tablespoon extra virgin olive oil

2 teaspoons cumin

1 teaspoon chili powder

1 teaspoon smoked paprika

1/2 teaspoon salt

1 teaspoon dried oregano

1 red bell pepper, cored and diced

1 (4 ounce) can diced green chilies, drained (or 1 jalapeno, diced)

1 cup corn kernels, fresh or frozen and defrosted

1 (15 ounce) can black beans, drained and rinsed

12 ounces salsa or enchilada sauce

1 and 1/2 cups cooked brown rice

1/2 cup shredded Monterey Jack cheese*

1/4 cup shredded cheddar cheese*

serving suggestions: fresh cilantro, diced green onions, avocado

## DIRECTIONS:

Start by warming the oil in a large skillet (mine is 3 quarts) over medium heat.

Add the onion and cook for 3 minutes, then add the spices (cumin to oregano) and stir together. Continue to cook for another 2-3 minutes.

Next add the red pepper and the green chilies and stir together. Cook for another 2-3 minutes then add the drained and rinsed beans, corn, salsa, and rice. Stir everything until well-combined.

Turn the oven to broil then top the mixture in the skillet with the shredded cheese.

Place the skillet in the oven and cook for about 3-4 minutes until the cheese is golden and bubbly on top.

Serve warm with diced green onions, cilantro, and/or avocado.

_____

_____

_____

_____

_____

_____

_____

_____

_____

_____

_____

_____

_____

_____

_____

_____

_____

_____

_____

_____

_____

_____

_____

# Day 5: Prayerful

## Today's Verse

*"While they are still talking about their needs, I will go ahead and answer their prayers!"* Isaiah 65:24 (NLT)

## Inspiration

Raising godly children in a world where spiritual warfare for their minds and souls is raging on every plane of existence can feel pretty much like going nose to nose with a speeding freight train.

But take this to heart, sweet mama, we're not helpless—not at all. There's something very real, very strong, and very proactive us mothers can do to defend and protect our precious children: we can pray.

Never, ever underestimate the inherent power of prayer. Praying is the most and the least we can do for these incredible beings that caused our hearts to leap outside our bodies when they were born and stay nestled in our embrace ever after.

"Well, what exactly should I pray?" you wonder.

I recommend Hot Fudge Verses—scriptures we can pour over our children. We moms are more than willing to storm the fiery gates of hell to remind the enemy who he's messing with.

But the best way to storm the gates of hell is by storming the gates of heaven.

What petitions could be more effective than the actual Word ordained by the Creator of the universe? *"For the word of God is living and powerful, and sharper than any two-edged sword..."* Hebrews 4:12 (NKJV).

Please, DO, take the time to search your Bible and compile your own go-to list of Hot Fudge Verses, but in the meantime, here are some of mine (remember, they're scriptures tailored as personalized prayers for each specific child):

**Hot Fudge Verses (to pour over your children and grands)**

Psalm 3:3 (NIV): *"You, Lord, are a shield around [child's name], bestow glory on him/her and lift up his/her head high."*

Psalm 25:16-17 (NASB) *"Turn to _____ and be gracious to him/her, for he/she is lonely and afflicted. The troubles of his/her heart are enlarged; Bring _____ out of his/her distresses."*

Psalm 138:8 (MSG) *"Finish what you started in _____, God. Your love is eternal—don't quit on him/her now."*

*Beauty Tip*

Running low on foundation? Mix what's left with a bit of moisturizer.

Don't forget to: Moisturize, moisturize, moisturize!

*Easy Meals for Busy Moms*

## QUESADILLAS

INGREDIENTS FOR THE SAUCE:

1 c. mayonnaise

3 tbsp. juice from jar of pickled jalapeños

3 tbsp. minced pickled jalapeños

2 tsp. garlic powder

2 tsp. cumin

2 tsp. paprika

1/2 tsp. cayenne

Kosher salt

FOR THE ASSEMBLY:

8 medium flour tortillas

4 c. shredded chicken

2 c. shredded Monterey Jack

12 slices American (or cheddar) cheese

## DIRECTIONS:

Make sauce: in a medium bowl, whisk together mayo, jalapeño juice, minced jalapeños, garlic powder, cumin, paprika, and cayenne. Season with kosher salt.

To another medium bowl, add chicken. Toss chicken with half of the quesadilla sauce. Set the rest aside for dipping.

In a large skillet over medium-high heat, add a flour tortilla. Top with 2 slices of American cheese and ½ cup chicken, then sprinkle with ½ cup Monterey Jack. Place second tortilla on top. Cook until the bottom tortilla is golden, about 2 minutes, then flip and cook until the second tortilla is golden and the cheese has melted, about 2 more minutes.

Repeat process with remaining ingredients to make 3 more quesadillas. Slice into wedges and serve warm with remaining sauce for dipping.

# Day 6: Equipped

## Today's Verse

*"Have I not commanded you? Be strong and courageous. Do not be afraid; do not be discouraged, for the LORD your God will be with you wherever you go."* Joshua 1:9 NIV

## INSPIRATION

Do you ever feel like God has called you to tasks that seem beyond your abilities? We all do. Some of us are blessed with special-needs children and sometimes that seems like more than we can handle. Some of us try to juggle a career, carpool, day care, dinner prep, grocery shopping—the list seems to never end. Some of us are dealing with very difficult medical needs and those situations seem all-consuming. When life feels overwhelming, we can remind ourselves that God has not forgotten us. He has equipped us.

We're guessing that Esther in the Bible felt overwhelmed too. She'd never been queen before, yet God saw her and appointed her to save her people. She was a simple orphan girl, but she had a big God who worked through her. God gave her courage to go before the king. God asked her to do something hard, and He equipped her for the task. Just like Esther we can be sure that God does not give us a hard task and then let us fend for ourselves. He walks with us and equips us.

God is patient with our attempts. Sometimes we feel like an insecure daughter, constantly calling to Him for help. Please know that He listens, and He answers your pleas.

As God boldly told Joshua, "Be strong and courageous. Do not be afraid; do not be discouraged, for the Lord your God will be with you wherever you go." We can rest in the promise that God is near to us as well. If God has called you to be a mom, He will carry you through.

**Prayer for Today**

God, I often feel overwhelmed when life gets crazy. Help me to rest in the assurance that You will give me what I need for each day. Bless me with Your peace, Your contentment and Your reassurance. May I remember You are Almighty God and rest in You. I trust You, Lord. In Jesus' name, Amen.

## *Beauty Tip*

Keep mascara from smudging and getting all over the place with a business card.

Use the card as a buffer between your eyelids & lashes.

## *Easy Meals for Busy Moms*

# One Pot Beef Spinach Soup

Ingredients:

1 pound ground beef

3 garlic cloves, minced

2 cartons (32 ounces each) reduced-sodium beef broth

2 cans (14-1/2 ounces each) diced tomatoes with green pepper, celery and onion, undrained

1 teaspoon dried basil

1/2 teaspoon pepper

1/2 teaspoon dried oregano

1/4 teaspoon salt

3 cups uncooked bow tie pasta

4 cups fresh spinach, coarsely chopped

Grated Parmesan cheese

## Directions:

In a 6-qt. stockpot, cook beef and garlic over medium heat until beef is no longer pink, breaking up beef into crumbles, 6-8 minutes; drain. Stir in broth, tomatoes and seasonings; bring to a boil. Stir in pasta; return to a boil. Cook, uncovered, until pasta is tender, 7-9 minutes.

Stir in spinach until wilted. Sprinkle servings with cheese.

_____

_____

_____

_____

_____

_____

_____

_____

_____

_____

_____

_____

_____

_____

_____

_____

_____

_____

_____

_____

_____

# Day 7: Fearless

## Today's Verse

*I sought the Lord, and He answered me; He delivered me from all my fears. Those who look to Him are radiant; their faces are never covered with shame.* Psalm 34:4-5 (NIV)

## Inspiration

If you ask Google, it will confirm there are 365 verses that tell us to fear not! I love our God! He is so detailed. One reminder for every day of the year.

If I gave you a hundred bucks, could you list 10 things that scare you in less than 30 seconds? I could! Fear is real. There are fears of every kind. Fear of bugs. Fear of heights. Fear of falling. Fear of failing. The list can go on and on.

Want to know a secret? The answer to ALL our fears is simply showing up before our Father. When we go before Him and tell Him about all the things that scare us, it also means we are spending time with Him. If we are spending time with Him, He rubs off on us. If He rubs off on us, we begin to shine brightly. When we shine brightly, we start to forget about the things that scare us. It might take 365 visits, but the Bible is clear, *"Those who look to Him are radiant."* Basically, not only does He make the fear disappear, but He also makes us radiant. Wow!

Friend, there is no fear too small or too great for our Father. Tell Him everything. You are fearless! You just might not know it YET.

**Prayer for Today**

Father, you tell us that we can be delivered from all our fears and those who look to You are radiant. I want that. I want to be fearless and radiant, and I am willing to go through the process. I will be patient and persistent in prayer. Thank You because You already see me that way. In Jesus' name, Amen.

*Beauty Tip*

Skip using makeup brushes and apply foundation and concealer with your fingers.

When you're short on time, don't waste seconds looking for the right brush — just use your fingers. And since your ring finger is the weakest, use it to blend creams ensuring a light touch.

## *Easy Meals for Busy Moms*

## Sausage Spaghetti Spirals

**Ingredients:**

1 pound bulk Italian sausage

1 medium green pepper, chopped

5 cups spiral pasta, cooked and drained

1 jar (24 ounces) spaghetti sauce

1-1/2 cups shredded part-skim mozzarella cheese

**Directions:**

In a large skillet, cook sausage and green pepper over medium heat until meat is no longer pink; drain. Stir in pasta and spaghetti sauce.

Transfer to a greased 13x9-in. baking dish. Cover and bake at 350° for 25 minutes. Uncover; sprinkle with cheese. Bake 5-10 minutes longer or until cheese is melted.

_____

_____

_____

_____

_____

_____

_____

_____

_____

_____

_____

_____

_____

_____

_____

_____

_____

_____

_____

_____

_____

_____

_____

_____

_____

_____

_____

_____

_____

_____

_____

_____

_____

_____

_____

_____

_____

_____

_____

_____

_____

_____

_____

_____

_____

_____

_____

_____

_____

_____

_____

_____

_____

_____

_____

_____

_____

_____

_____

_____

_____

_____

_____

_____

_____

_____

_____

_____

_____

_____

_____

_____

_____

_____

_____

_____

_____

_____

_____

_____

_____

_____

_____

_____

_____

_____

_____

_____

_____

_____

_____

_____

_____

_____

_____

_____

_____

_____

_____

_____

_____

_____

_____

_____

_____

_____

_____

_____

_____

_____

_____

_____

_____

_____

_____

_____

_____

_____

_____

_____

_____

_____

_____

_____

_____

_____

_____

_____

_____

_____

_____

_____

_____

_____

_____

_____

_____

_____

_____

_____

_____

_____

_____

_____

Made in the USA
Coppell, TX
01 May 2021

54817044R00028